ABetterImpact.How
Copyright © 2022
Kassidy Coleman & Jacob Sequeira

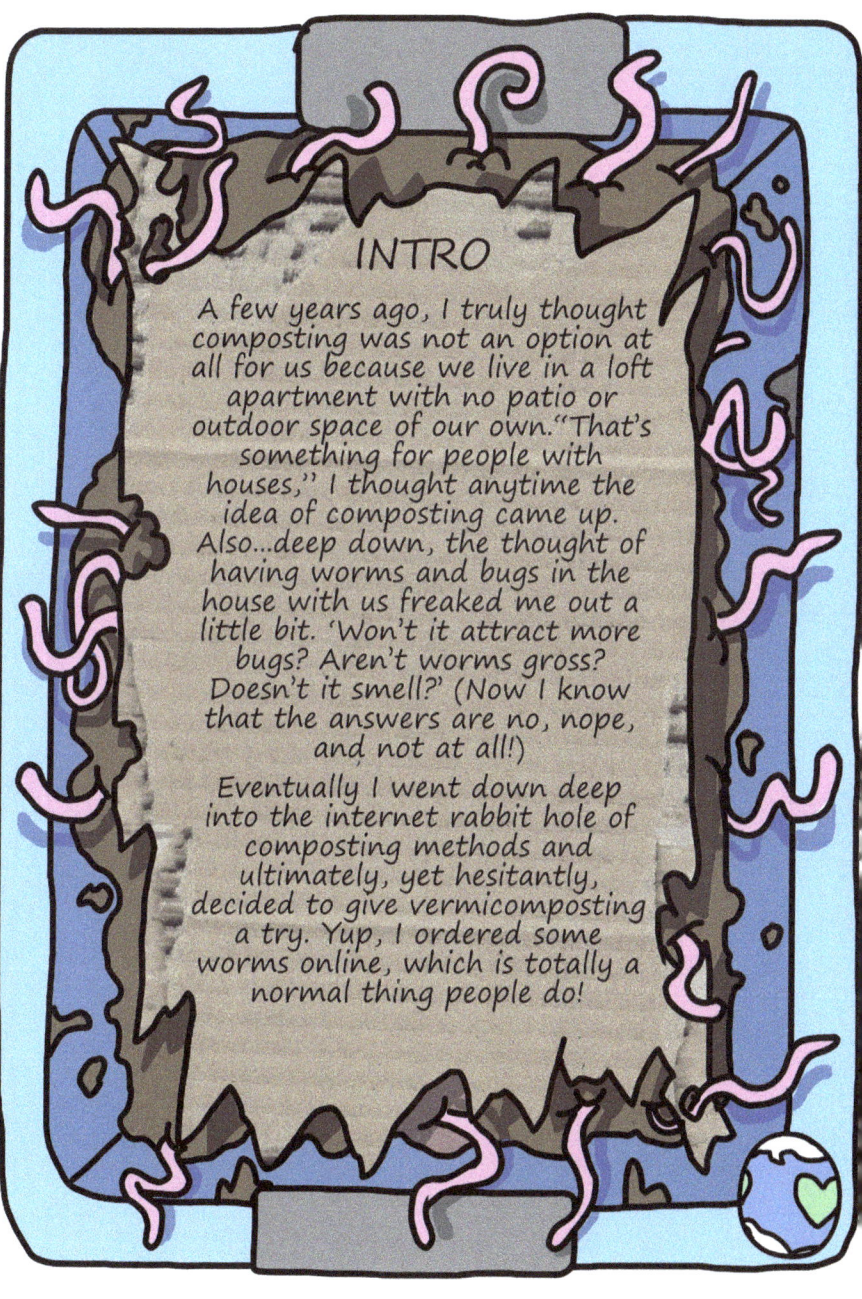

INTRO

A few years ago, I truly thought composting was not an option at all for us because we live in a loft apartment with no patio or outdoor space of our own. "That's something for people with houses," I thought anytime the idea of composting came up. Also...deep down, the thought of having worms and bugs in the house with us freaked me out a little bit. 'Won't it attract more bugs? Aren't worms gross? Doesn't it smell?' (Now I know that the answers are no, nope, and not at all!)

Eventually I went down deep into the internet rabbit hole of composting methods and ultimately, yet hesitantly, decided to give vermicomposting a try. Yup, I ordered some worms online, which is totally a normal thing people do!

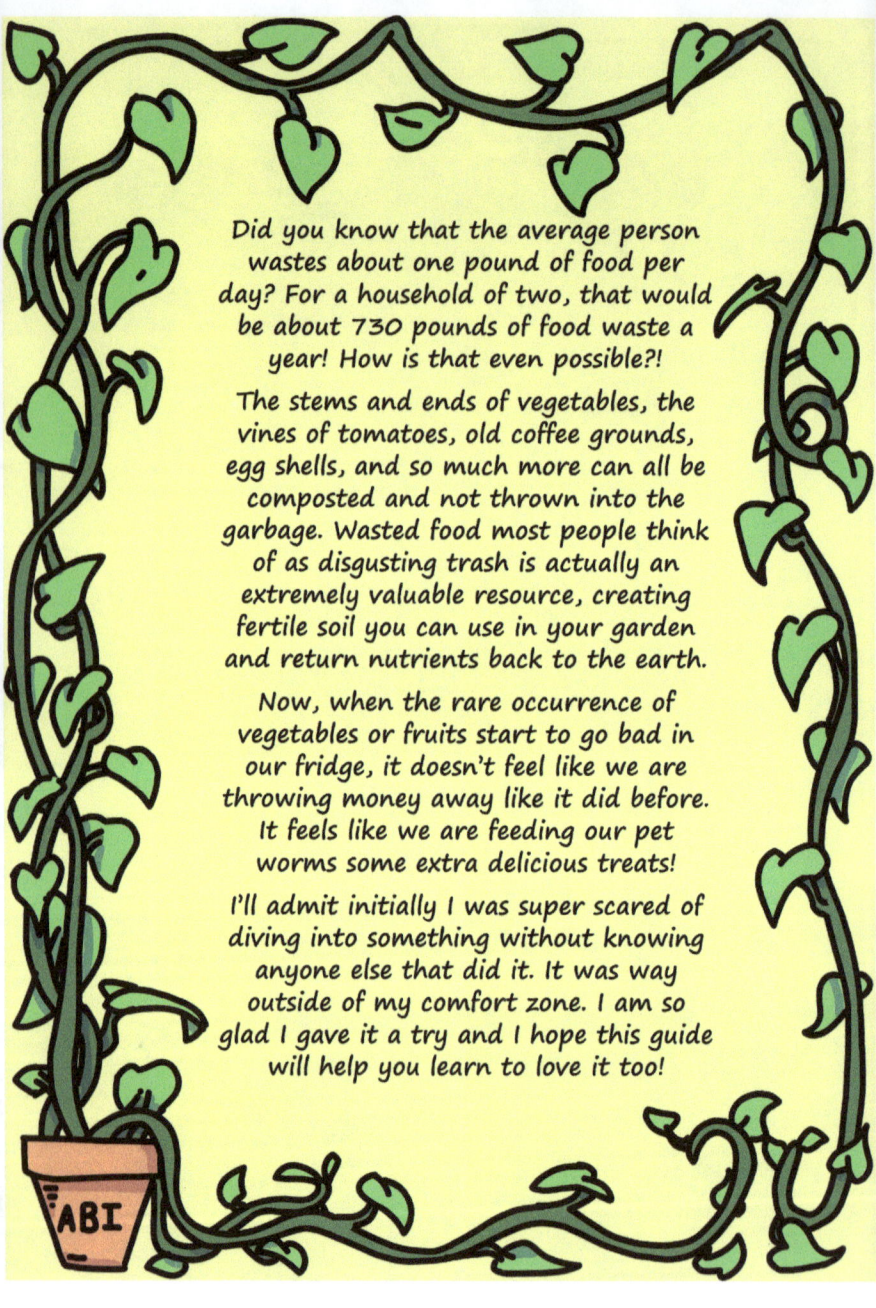

Did you know that the average person wastes about one pound of food per day? For a household of two, that would be about 730 pounds of food waste a year! How is that even possible?!

The stems and ends of vegetables, the vines of tomatoes, old coffee grounds, egg shells, and so much more can all be composted and not thrown into the garbage. Wasted food most people think of as disgusting trash is actually an extremely valuable resource, creating fertile soil you can use in your garden and return nutrients back to the earth.

Now, when the rare occurrence of vegetables or fruits start to go bad in our fridge, it doesn't feel like we are throwing money away like it did before. It feels like we are feeding our pet worms some extra delicious treats!

I'll admit initially I was super scared of diving into something without knowing anyone else that did it. It was way outside of my comfort zone. I am so glad I gave it a try and I hope this guide will help you learn to love it too!

ABI

COMPOSTING

What is it?

Composting is the natural process of turning food scraps & organic waste into nutrient-rich fertilizer.

The end result can be used to feed your home garden and indoor plants, or simply to have a better impact on the planet.

This guide will focus on the composting method called **vermicomposting,** which utilizes worms to aid the process of decomposition.

You don't need any special skills or tools to compost, anyone can do it!

We need more people to try (even just a little) to have a better impact on the planet

Why Should I?!

Any time you throw out trash in a plastic bag, it gets sent to a heaping landfill. Your trash will sit there for a very long time and not decompose properly. Landfills are not designed to do anything more than store trash.

According to the EPA, food scraps and yard waste currently make up more than 30% of what we throw away and could be composted instead. Everyone and anyone should compost.

Other valid reasons to compost:

 1) Easy, practically free way to get all-natural fertilizer for your plants and garden

2) No more smelly trash or pests

 3) You won't have to take your trash out as often

Living in a small Space?
YOU can still compost!

Vermicomposting works in a multitude of living situations.

not comfortable with worms? you still have options!

- Locate a community garden that has a compost collection bin.
- Find a local composting service that picks up scraps (a quick online search of "composting" + your city name should bring up results)
- Check with your local farmers at your farmers markets and see if they are willing to take your scraps off your hands
- You can also look into the bokashi method

A couple of keywords to understand BEFORE STARTING

GREENS - The food waste you will be adding to your compost. This includes, but is not limited to: Fruit & vegetable scraps (even if it is moldy), coffee grounds and tea bags (remove the staple), bread, cereal, rice, beans, lentils, garden clippings & cut/recently pulled weeds.
This is what your worms will eat and where your compost will get its nutrients.

BROWNS - You will add "browns" any time you add greens to your bin. This adds carbon, absorbs moisture, and keeps the compost from getting too smelly! Some examples of "browns" are: Shredded newspaper, cut up paper bags and pizza boxes, dry pasta, and usually whatever you sweep up off the floor/vacuum up (hair and crumbs).

A good rule of thumb is to have twice the amount of browns to greens.

SCRAPS

"Scraps" are the organic waste you add to your compost. Usually it is food waste that you would have otherwise thrown in the garbage.

WORM CASTINGS

The final result of the composting process. Essentially, it is a nice way of saying worm poop. This is what you will add to your garden to provide nutrients.

How do I START?

Setting up a worm bin is easy and relatively cheap. You can get most of the materials at your local hardware store or online. This can be done in a house or apartment - indoors or outdoors. We use this method in our apartment that has no private outdoor space and have also built a few for friends and family with various living situations. Once you have the materials, setting up will take no more than an hour.

What you will need:

- Storage tote or bucket (not clear)
- Power drill
- Dirt (potting soil, vegetable garden mix, coco-coir, any dirt will do)
- Red Wiggler composting worms
- Shredded newspaper (not glossy)/cardboard
- Composting food scraps

For our home composting setup, we use an 18 gallon storage tote. If you don't cook much at home, you may be able to get away with using a 5 gallon bucket. We have built "Composting Starter Kits" for people in 5 gallon buckets and some have since upgraded and others have been happy with the size – it is all a very personal choice. Do what works best for you!

Step 1 - Drill holes around the perimeter

Step 2 - Add a thick layer of dirt, filling about ⅓ of the container

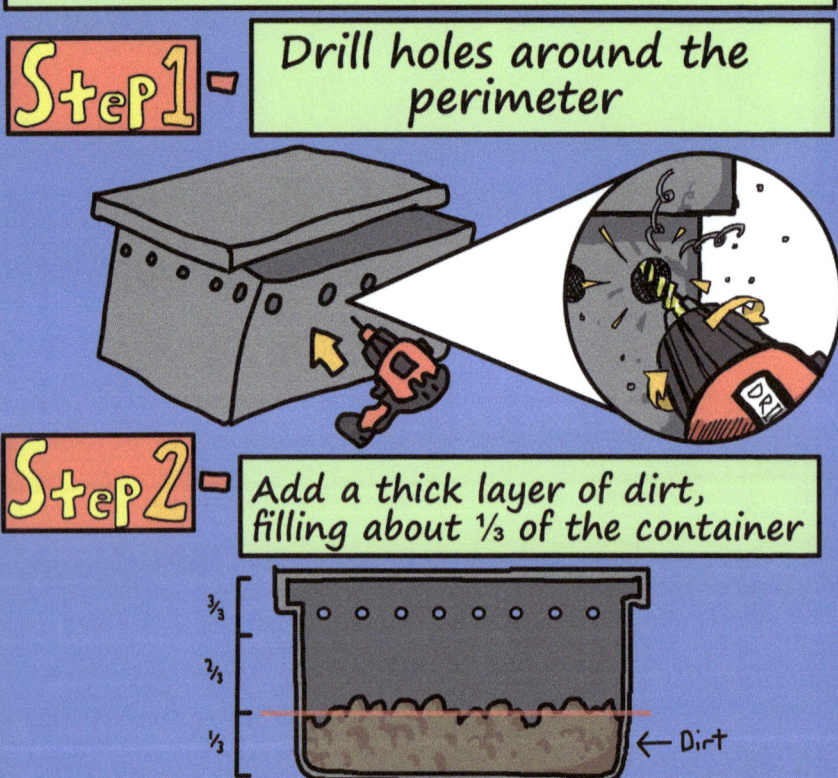

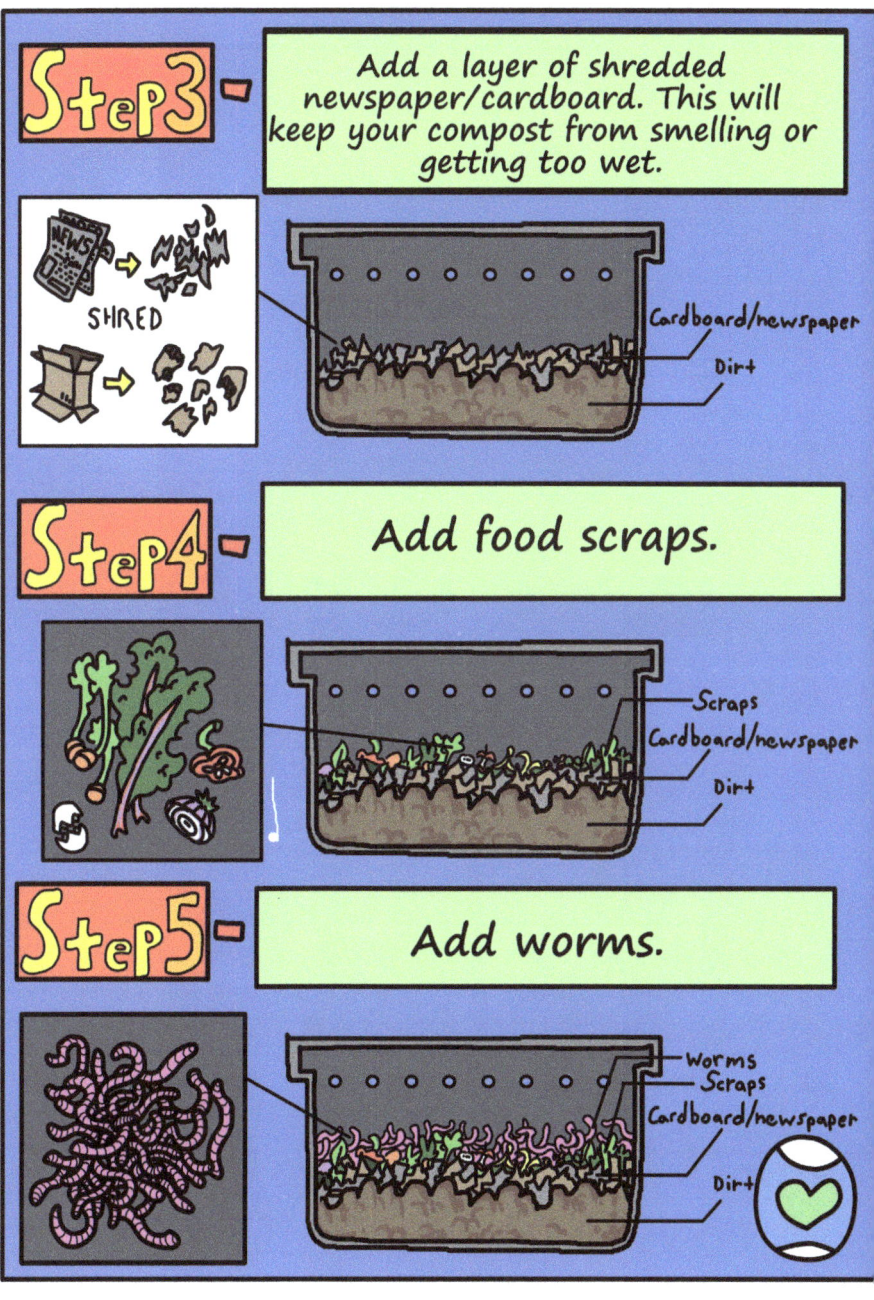

Step 6

Add another thin layer of dirt, covering the scraps and worms.

Initially, you probably want your container to be a little more than half full. It does not have to be any exact measurement. As the worms eat, your pile will grow.

ゲト!

COMPLETED COMPOST BIN!

COMMON HOUSEHOLD
ITEMS TO COMPOST

- Fruit and vegetable scraps (always remember to remove the produce sticker!)
- Coffee grounds and filters
- Old spices and herbs
- Tea (some tea bags can be composted, just make sure it does not contain plastic and remove any staples!)
- Leftover wine, liquor, & beer
- Grass & plant clippings
- Raked leaves
- Shredded paper & cardboard
- 100% cotton balls
- Used paper towels and napkins
- Tissues
- Egg shells

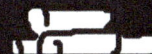

TOP 5 WEIRD things you can (and should) COMPOST!

Composting isn't just for food scraps! Did you know you can and **should** compost these things? Enrich your soil with vital nutrients and avoid sending more things to the landfill!

1st - BOOGERS & SNOT.

Blow your nose in a tissue?

Obviously the more sustainable option would be to use a reusable handkerchief, there will always be circumstances where you end up with a paper tissue to quickly blow or pick your nose. This is not recommended though if the tissue is covered with snot from being truly sick (i.e. cold or flu).

2nd - EARWAX

Did you hear that? Earwax can be composted.

Use a tissue or cotton ball to quickly clean your ear? Go ahead and throw it in the compost. If you use a 100% organic cotton swab to clean out earwax, that can be composted too. Make sure to check if your swab is 100% cotton as some brands, unfortunately, do have plastic on the ends.

HAIR

Do an at home hair cut? Trim your bangs or beard? Shave your head or...somewhere else?

While it is not advised to compost chemically treated (bleached, dyed, permed, etc) hair, untreated hair can be a wonderful addition to your compost. Hair is extremely high in nitrogen and will add beneficial nutrients to your soil.

HERBIVOROUS PET POO

Don't compost dog or cat poop because there will be a high risk of parasites. But you 100% can compost your herbivorous pets' poop and gain some extremely fertile soil. Rabbits, guinea pigs, chinchillas, and hamsters are practically mini fertilizer factories!

FINGER NAILS

Clip your nails?

As long as you don't have any nail polish on them, both your toenails and fingernails can be thrown in the compost bin! Just like hair, it can be a great source of nutrients to your compost heap.

Honorable Mentions:

Floss - Unfortunately most floss is usually made of nylon and can't be composted. Next time you need to buy some floss, consider looking for an eco-friendly brand that can be! Usually compostable floss is made from silk or plant fibers.

Pee - We don't recommend doing this if you have a small indoor compost bin like ours, but if you have an outdoor bin or heap, pee can actually be beneficial to your compost.

WHAT CAN'T BE COMPOSTED

Meat & Dairy
Can attract pests and make your compost smell.

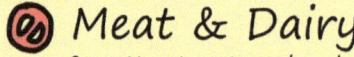

Dog, Cat, or human Feces
Can contain parasites.

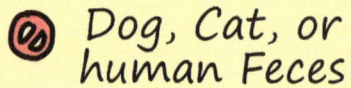

Fat, oil, or grease
Can cause odor problems and attract unwanted pests

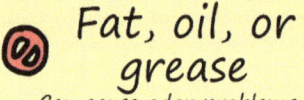

Coal or charcoal

Can be harmful to plants

Diseased plants
Diseases & plant pests can survive and be transferred to your plants

Anything not organic

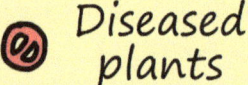

When in doubt, throw it out!

Think tending to compost is tough?
It's NOT! Don't freak out, we gotchu :)

How to Care
FOR
YOUR COMPOST

LEAVE IT ALONE!

This is <u>not</u> something you have to be checking everyday. We fill ours about once a week with our kitchen scraps from cooking and that is sufficient.

Allow the decomposition process to happen.

A Properly Balanced Compost Bin Won't:

1. **Smell bad** – It will smell like something, but not an offensive odor. When you lift the lid, it should smell like a bag of dirt you would buy at the store.

2. **Be wet** – When you grab a clump of compost, it should be a malleable handful of dirt that does not fall apart.

3. **Attract pests** – Burying your scraps in the dirt should ensure no pests are attracted.

HARVESTING

Want to collect your worm castings? Start feeding your worms to one side! In a few weeks most of the worms should have migrated to the side you have been putting the food. Here are two methods we have used to harvest our compost:

METHOD 1

Use a designated colander or sifter to separate the remaining worms from your compost.

METHOD 2

Set newspaper on the ground and make multiple small cone shaped piles of the compost on it. Worms don't like light, so they will start to leave.

FAQs
Frequently asked questions

Q: Can I compost something labeled as "biodegradable"?

A: "Biodegradable" simply means that the item has been produced in a way to have the ability to break down in the environment. While it may be true that it can break down in the world if you throw it out, it can still take a significant amount of time. Try not to add things labeled as "biodegradable" to your compost bin because it will just take up space and will not provide any benefit to it.

Q: Will the worms escape?

A: Nope! Just keep the lid on and these worms will stay where you feed them.

Q: How often should I feed the worms?

A: Ideally, about 1-2 times a week. If you miss a week here and there, the worms will be fine. Luckily, these are "pets" that you don't have to hire a pet sitter for if you go on vacation.

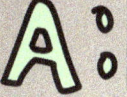

FAQ Continued

Q: Where should I keep my scraps while waiting to compost them?

A: This is totally up to you! You can purchase a compost pail and keep it on your counter or under your sink. Another option is to designate a container and keep it in your fridge. It really does not matter! All that matters is that you are composting.

Scraps

Storage Bin

Q: Can something labeled "commercially compostable" be added to the bin?

A: You may have come across something that resembles plastic, but is labeled "commercially compostable". These will break down in a worm bin, but it may take some time. If you want to compost a "commercially compostable" plastic, we highly suggest cutting it up first to help it break down faster.

Q: My compost bin STINKS! What should I do?

A: If your compost bin smells, add some additional shredded cardboard or leaves to it and leave it alone for a few days. Most likely your browns to green ratio was off the last time you added scraps.

Worm Tea

Eliminate the use of chemicals in your garden by making some delicious and nutritious worm tea for your plants. Extremely rich with calcium, nitrogen, phosphorus, and potassium. This is a great alternative to chemical fertilizers and if you have a vermicompost bin, it is free!

You will need:

- 2 cups worm castings from your compost
- 1 gallon of water
- A jar or bucket
- Cheese cloth or rag

Take 2 cups of worm castings from your compost and add it directly to a jar with 1 gallon of water. If you plan to add this to a sprayer or something with a very fine nozzle, we suggest putting the castings in a cheese cloth or tying it up in a rag cut from an old t-shirt. Otherwise, it may clog up the nozzle and be hard to disperse. Let it steep overnight and give it a good stir.

This is highly concentrated fertilizer, so you can dilute it into water in a watering can and water your plants with it as usual. If you want to give a plant an extra boost, add the worm tea directly to your plant undiluted.

Ideally use within 1 week. Can be stored at room temperature.

SOME COOL FACTS
about WORMS

- Worms are able to eat their weight every day

- The longest worm ever recorded was 22 feet long. That's taller than 3 Shaqs!

- There are 2,700 different kinds of earthworms.

- Worms reproduce on their own! If you are feeding them a healthy diet, they will reproduce baby worms to help eat the scraps. A well maintained compost bin should not need any extra worms added for years.

About A Better IMPACT.

Hey! Thanks for checking out our composting guide. Our names are Jacob and Kassidy. We currently live in Richmond, VA with our two dogs and guinea pig.

We met 10 years ago and have been inseparable ever since. Growing together, we slowly became more conscious of what we consume and how our life impacts the planet. We started A Better Impact as a blog to encourage and inform people of small changes anyone can make to have a better impact on earth.

Other than our passion for the environment, we are also creatives!

Kassidy is a plant and indoor gardening hobbyist and loves to cook vegan food.

Jacob is an artist focusing on drawing, and also loves reading manga and listening to music

Our goal is to ultimately make the sustainable and eco-friendly lifestyle easy and accessible to everyone. We hope to raise awareness of the impact people have on the environment.

More things you can compost

- Anything labeled "compostable"
- Bamboo toothbrush (remove bristles first)
- Cardboard boxes
- Cardboard pizza boxes
- Coffee grounds
- Crumbs from packaged snacks
- Crumbs you sweep from the floor (remove anything inorganic)
- Dirt
- Dryer lint (only if you wear 100% natural clothing)
- Dust bunnies
- Egg cartons (cardboard)
- Eggshells
- Flowers from floral arrangements after they die
- Food scraps
- Fruits
- Grass clippings
- Hair (not chemically treated)
- Hay and straw
- House plants
- Latex
- Leaves
- Left over beer & wine
- Loose leaf tea
- Moldy food
- Nail clippings

Even more things to compost

- Nut shells
- Old bread
- Old spices
- Paper
- Paper coffee filters
- Paper cupcake & muffin liners
- Paper shopping bags
- Paper towel rolls
- Pencil shavings
- Pet hair
- Saw dust (untreated wood)
- Shredded Newspaper (not glossy)
- Stale chips
- Tea bags (make sure they are all-natural cotton or hemp)
- Tissue paper gift wrap (no glitter)
- Toilet paper rolls
- Urine
- Used matches
- Used napkins and paper towels
- Vegetables
- Vegetarian Animal Poop (guinea pigs, hamsters, rabbits, etc)
- Wine corks
- Wooden chopsticks
- Wooden toothpicks
- Yard trimmings

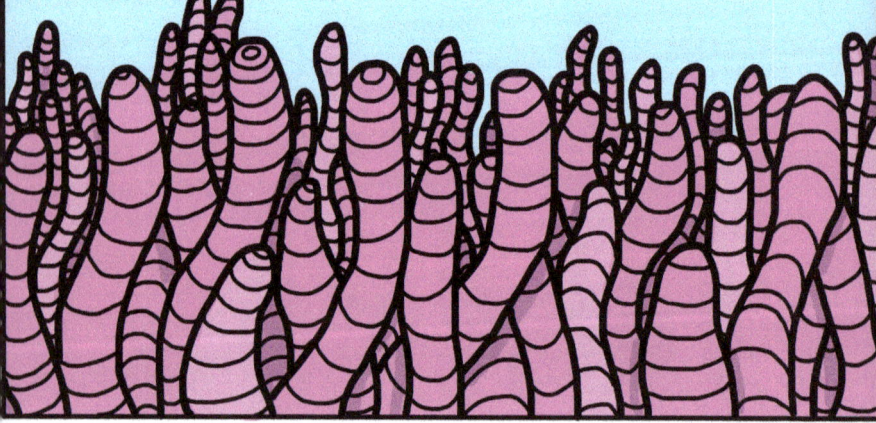

www.ingramcontent.com/pod-product-compliance
Lightning Source LLC
Chambersburg PA
CBHW051651120626
46551CB00015B/2316